WHAT HAPPENS AFTER

#MeToo

Tackling the Iceberg

Dr. Laila Risgallah Wahba

Contents

CONTENTS

Acknowledgment

M any people have contributed to this book seeing the light.

First and foremost, thank you, Wahid Wahba, my husband and my prime supporter and encourager. Thank you for believing in me even when things were unclear in my own mind. Thank you for supporting my crazy entrepreneurial spirit.

Thank you, Teo van der Weele, for your leadership at the Middle East School of Sexual Abuse Related Pastoral Counseling. Thank you for helping me at times when faith was too hard in the face of the atrocities we studied and saw. You taught me to look at the cross when things got rough.

Thank you, Vibeke Moeller, for asking over and over again, "How will you take care of yourself?" when at times all I wanted to do was to allow victims to crawl all over me, leaving me drained and exhausted. Thank you for teaching me how to take care of myself as a counselor.

Thank you, Eric Spady, for your training on

delicate and intricate subjects, yet treating them so respectfully and elegantly. I have learned so much from you.

About the author

L aila Risgallah was born in Cairo, Egypt, and is passionate about children and their welfare. She is a pediatrician with a master's degree in pediatrics and a doctorate in childhood studies and practiced medicine for nearly two decades. In 2009, she decided to equip herself to abolish sexual abuse and bullying. She studied for the Middle East Sexual Abuse Related Pastoral Counseling diploma, a three-year certificate program, and graduated in 2012. She is known for her Christian youth TV program, We Will Live our Lives Well, seen by an audience of 40 million Arabic speakers each week in the Middle East, North Africa, Canada, and the U.S.

Laila is founder and president of Not Guilty, which works toward abolishing sexual abuse and bullying. She is an Ashoka Fellow, an inspirational public speaker, author, and determined social advocate. She is passionate about strong leadership and empowering others. Her determined mission is to be a voice for the unheard and fight against sexual abuse in society. She created the first ever anti-sexual-abuse mobile app for kids, S.K.I.T., and is a faculty member with the Haggai Institute for Advanced Leadership Training. She is married to Wahid and has two sons.

Foreword

As a founder myself of a global anti-risk organization in 54 countries sitting on panels working closely with law enforcement, medical, legal, social work, government and more... I often get asked «What one thing would you change to address risk?»

I love to address laws, medical and educational professionals and more. But, I truly believe left to only one thing to address risk, the resounding answer is «THE FAMILY.» When I speak to a thousand lawyers, doctors or the senate, this addresses a problem already out of control. The family on the other hand is the preventative magic. While no parent can prevent all pain and abuse, they are the single most influential component intentionally or unintentionally in a child to adult life. Lawyers, doctors, government, FBI, police can talk all day about how to respond. The family creates the petrie dish a child is grown from.

Dr. Laila´s booklet is practical advice for parents. In lay terms it gives a handle on every parent´s worst nightmare with simple tools to see, address and build resilience in the face of whatever comes.

There is likely no child in the world that has not faced some level of harassment, demeaning or bullying. We can not assume our children will never face a predator. The goal is to for them to stand strong in the face of attack with courage, resilience and power to protect themselves or run to a circle of protection that will understand, guide and provide unconditional love in the face of pain. Life is broken. This booklet is a good start toward helping our children navigate a world of abuse that´s ongoing and ever changing.

I have known Dr. Laila for a long time. She courageously has dared to address these issues professionally in a context even more conservative than our Western world. She has been the tip of the spear in the Middle East foraging into a taboo subject making it safe for the wounded to come to a doctor, a mommy, a leader who cares more about them and their healing and safety than being culturally correct. This is what it takes to break into these broken taboos shattering the silence. As a founder that began building programs in cultures where silence was mandatory, I know the power of being the «voice of the silenced.» I know the price you pay for doing this. Dr. Laila has done this and now is attempting to give professional but nurturing guidance to parents in the fight to raise radiant sons and daughters wherever the darkness threatens.

Rebecca McDonald
President & Founder
Women At Risk, International
www.warinternational.org

Introduction

We live in a distressing time. Headlines remind us constantly of things we don't want to see: victims who were exploited and abused by more powerful or manipulative people, offenders who have gotten away with their abuses for far too many years, and a culture that has turned a blind eye to some of its most vulnerable members. These are signs of serious social and psychological problems, and we wish we didn't have to deal with them.

But seeing these things is better than not seeing them, and dealing with them is better than leaving them alone. We have to know what the problems are in order to fix them, and as painful as they can be, knowing them is the first step toward a solution.

This book is an important part of the solution. It not only identifies the problem of abuse; it also equips parents and others who work with children and youth to guard against abuse, recognize its signs, and prepare young people to live in a threatening world. It acknowledges the importance of the #MeToo movement while helping parents and children reduce the number of voices that will ever have to say "me too." It brings things that were secret into the light.

If you have children, work with them, or know victims of abuse of any age, read this book. Arm yourself with the knowledge to prepare hearts, expose lies, and heal wounds. Yes, these times are distressing, but there are solutions. This is one of them. It educates us about things we don't want to see so that maybe we can see them a lot less often.

—*Chris Tiegreen, author*

1

What's the Weather Like Today?

Actress Alyssa Milano tweeted, "If you've been sexually harassed or assaulted write 'me too' as a reply to this tweet," and it quickly turned into a movement. That was October 15, 2017, and the next morning, close to 40,000 people—mostly but not exclusively women—had replied.

The words "me too" flooded social media, surprising many who may have assumed that sexual harassment and assault are isolated incidents. The posts made a clear statement that our culture has often turned the other way and is only beginning to understand how pervasive this problem can be.

And as one person tweeted, "#MeToo is just the tip of the iceberg. There are millions without any computer or Internet access who have worse experiences of daily abuse.

"#MeToo won the person of the year for 2017.[1] How could a hashtag win person of the year[2]? How many people were just waiting for something like this hashtag before they would pour out the secret they had been keeping for days, months, years, or even decades?

#MeToo is just the tip of the iceberg

Women, men, and children could at last tell the secret they had been carrying, the secret that changed their lives forever, the secret that made them see the world forever in a different light: a world that cannot be trusted.

This secret of having been sexually harassed or assaulted raises all kinds of questions, both about the secret itself and the secrecy surrounding it: why would anyone who has been sexually harassed or assaulted keep this secret? Why wouldn't they report it immediately? Who is the predator and what does he or she look like? What are the signs of abuse, assault, or harassment? What are the consequences? And finally, how can we protect our kids?

1-Christen A. Johnson and KT Hawbaker, "#MeToo: A Timeline of Events," in the Chicago Tribune, published online April 9, 2018. Accessed April 14, 2018, at http://www.chicagotribune.com/lifestyles/ct-me-too-timeline-20171208-htmlstory.html

2-"The Silence Breakers," Time magazine, Dec. 18, 2017.

This book is for every concerned parent, social worker, caregiver, teacher, and healthcare professioal who works with children. It is to help us "check the weather" with our children's moods and behaviors so we can be aware of what is going on in their lives.

#MeToo, the viral awareness campaign that inspired millions of posts on Facebook and Twitter, did not begin with Alyssa Milano, and it did not start in 2017. More than a decade ago, Tarana Burke identified the power of the phrase "me too" as one that could help women. She founded the Me Too movement in 2006 because she had experienced sexual assault and wanted to do something to help women and girls who had also survived sexual violence.

Then we heard about people like Jerry Sandusky at Penn State, or, as the #MeToo movement was growing in popularity, about Dr. Larry Nassar, the Olympic doctor who abused more than 200 girls under the pretext of treating them. As his trial was coming to a head, prominent actresses and actors brought their experiences of abuse into the light, many of which they had suffered at the hands of powerful people in the entertainment industry years ago. Many people began to see just how widespread the problem is.

So what are we as parents going to do about it? A hashtag is a great start for awareness, but it isn't enough to provoke change. The real battle goes well beyond awareness into understanding the problem and knowing how to respond. We cannot afford to ignore allegations until the next #MeToo or the next Larry Nassar appears. Nor should we as parents have to live in constant fear and anxiety for our children. We can no longer remain oblivious, choose denial, and tell ourselves that it can never happen to our children.

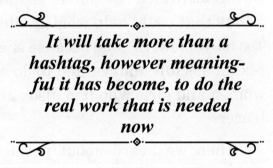

It will take more than a hashtag, however meaningful it has become, to do the real work that is needed now

As a pediatrician with a Ph.D. in childhood studies, I have helped hundreds of parents put their minds to rest concerning this issue. I have helped hundreds of parents rest assured that their kids are made aware of the dangers around them without making them fearful. I have helped many parents protect their kids from the nightmare of sexual abuse.

One parent I had trained using S.K.I.T method communicated to her 6-year-old daughter all I taught her. A few days later, when she was visiting a friend, she suddenly noticed that her daughter had disappeared. Her friend's 14-year-old son had disappeared too.

She frantically went looking for her daughter and found one of the rooms locked with the key. She could hear her daughter shout, "No, my mommy told me this is wrong. I will tell my mommy." Sure enough, the 14-year-old was attempting to molest the 6-year-old. He never expected her to be so well informed and ready to defend herself against the abuse. If we raise our children's awareness and teach them how to react, they will be able to handle these situations. If not, they will often freeze if someone tries to molest them.

"Mommy, I told him 'no' like you taught me," the girl asked. "Mommy, are you angry with me? Am I a bad girl?" If that mother had not attended my training, her daughter would have been a victim of sexual abuse today with all its repercussions—guilt, shame, fear, and emotional wounds that can last a lifetime.

Most of us not only fear for the safety of our kids; we also dread their questions. So what are we supposed to tell them? We do not want to open their eyes to the shameful things people do or make them afraid of everyone they meet. Maybe you are shy about discussing such touchy subjects with your kids because you do not know what their reaction will be. Perhaps you worry they might ask you a question you cannot answer. I have heard many reasons: "I'm afraid of losing my kids"; "I don't want them to be unpopular or unsociable"; "I dread failing them." These are all real concerns.

As a graduate of a three-year anti-sexual abuse certificate and winner of the Ashoka prize for social entrepreneurs, I have trained more than 4,000 parents and 9,000 children using my innovative S.K.I.T method. I spoke at Stanford University in 2015 about this method, which has been eye-opening for many.

One mother told me she had been reluctant to answer her daughter's questions. She did not want to expose her daughter to sexual subjects before she was ready. After the training, this mother began speaking openly to her little girl, using the S.K.I.T method. If our children ask, they are ready to hear. We need to answer their questions and to earn their trust. It is time for more than a hashtag.

2

Beauty and the Beast: Profile of a Predator

"Know your enemy" is a well-known military principle. It applies to sports too; professional athletes watch their opponents' matches to learn how to strike at points of weakness and win the next game. We as parents need to have a similar approach toward sexual abuse—to study the tactics that the abuser uses and beat him at his own game. If we want to protect our children from sexual abuse, we need to learn who predators actually are.

In 87 percent of cases, the predator is someone known and liked by the child. He (or she) can be a parent, a relative, a neighbor, a friend of the family, a teacher, or even a doctor. He can be the guy who rents your basement or the neighbor you leave your kids with. Abusers are among the ordinary people we meet in our daily lives. They can come from any religious or ethnic background. Many times they are very well-respected figures in society. They have their own businesses, play sports, and have friends. They are often considered charming people.

But a predator is also a master manipulator. He does not start with the abuse but begins by grooming his victims, winning their trust and the confidence of their family. When the abuse starts, the child or teen is not sure whether what happened was planned or accidental. The victim doubts him- or herself because the predator is a respected person. In fact, the predator might be the only friend the child has. The child is too frightened to say anything because he or she knows the parents like the abuser. The child does not want to be accused of lying or creating drama.

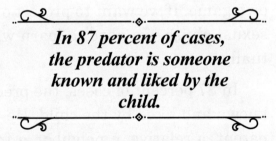

In 87 percent of cases, the predator is someone known and liked by the child.

Rachael Denhollander, one of the Olympic gymnasts who reported having been abused by Larry Nassar, described this process well:

Larry Nassar meticulously groomed me to exploit me for his sexual gain. He engaged in degrading and humiliating sex acts without my consent or permission. And Larry enjoyed it.. . . As we were being sexually violated even as very young children, as young as 6 years old, Larry was aroused by our humiliation and our pain. He asked us how it felt because he wanted to know.

At age 15, when I suffered from chronic back pain, Larry sexually assaulted me repeatedly under the guise of medical treatment for nearly a year. He did this with my mother in the room, carefully and perfectly obstructing her view so she would not know what he was doing. His ability to gain my trust and the trust of my parents, his grooming and carefully calculated brazen sexual assault was the result of deliberate, premeditated, intentional, and methodological patterns of abuse—patterns that were rehearsed long before I walked through Larry's exam room door and which continue to be perpetrated I believe on a daily basis for 16 more years, until I filed the police report. Larry is the most dangerous type of abuser. One who is capable of manipulating his victims through coldly calculated grooming methodologies, presenting the most wholesome, caring external persona as a deliberate means to ensure a steady stream of children to assault.[3]

Abusers may be found anywhere you find children or teens. They have positioned themselves near potential victims. They can be friends, relatives, or trusted professionals, male or female. There is not one specific profile.

The predator often finds his or her victim by choosing the more vulnerable children: the kid whose parents are constantly fighting; whose mother or father is addicted to drugs or alcohol; whose mother or father is suffering from cancer and is often absent; who has no friends at school; whose parents drive him ruthlessly, whether in school or in sports; who has a disability; or who is being raised in a single-parent home. Not all victims fit all of these descriptions; Nassar's victims, for example, often did not. But many times, children in vulnerable family situations become the easiest targets.

Abusers dazzle kids by keeping state-of-the-art toys and entertainment in their homes. They present themselves as a "friend" the child can trust and talk to, or as the child's "secret-keeper" who is trustworthy with personal and private matters. The predator becomes to your child everything you as a parent are not.

3- Natalie Musumeci, "Nassar's Sex Abuse Victims 'So Thankful' for Harsh Sentence," New York Post, January 24, 2018. Accessed April 14, 2018, at https://nypost.com/2018/01/24/nassars-sex-abuse-victims-so-thankful-for-harsh-sentence.

One day as I was training a single moms group on how to protect their kids against sexual abuse, a young mother approached me and told me that her 9-year-old son had been losing a lot of weight. He had a physical check-up, and nothing was wrong. I asked if her son played any sport, and she immediately began to falter. "He used to go swimming, but one day he came out of the pool and was very distressed. He told me that the coach touched him in his private parts more than once during the training. I told him that he was making a big fanfare out of nothing, and forced him to go to training the next day. He said the abuse happened again. He left the pool and decided never to go back to swimming. He is such a sissy."

I was sad when I heard this story. This mother has made her son an excellent candidate for further abuse, and to make matters worse, he will probably never tell his mother if it happens again because he believes she will not take his complaints seriously and protect him. She never confronted the coach or reported the incident, and she lost the trust of her son.

Predators have a high interest in kids, though they often try to hide it. They win the trust of the parents and perhaps offer to babysit while the parents go on a date night or offer to take the kids to the park. Of course, plenty of offers to babysit or take kids to the park are perfectly legitimate. Not everyone who does these things is an abuser. Most are not. But these are the tactics abusers use. Never be too trusting when an older teenager or adult is more interested in spending time with younger kids than with peers of their own age. Why would a 25-year-old be interested in a 12-year-old? That rarely makes sense except in the context of possible abuse.

Two friends came to visit me at my home. After dinner, as we were having dessert, one of them said, "I think a girl in my class is being abused, and I don't know what to do about it." She explained that an 8-year-old girl told her of a family friend who took her out to the park two or three times a week, bought her expensive gifts, and even offered to teach her how to drive—an 8-year-old! She felt so special and grown up. But as he was teaching her how to drive, he started touching her in a way that made her feel very uncomfortable. She didn't want to tell her mother because she loved the attention. We discussed some plans so she could encourage the girl totell her mother about the abuse that was happening.

Predators also try to find jobs that will get them close to children or teens on a regular basis. These can include work as a teacher, a babysitter, a school bus driver, a camp counselor, a dentist, a doctor, a music teacher, or a coach.

Many abusers are great at sports, games, and computer gaming, and will use any of these activities to groom and abuse their victims—even including blackmail and threats. They will give a child particular attention, prefer the child to others, and buy gifts for more than just special occasions. All these tactics are used to isolate the child away from his or her peers, thus making him or her an easy target.

Again, the recent case of Larry Nassar provides an example. According to the testimony of many of the girls he was convicted of abusing, he gave them gifts, invited them to his house, took care of them when they were injured, and gave them nicknames. Many of these young women considered him to be their advocate, a medical guru who would relieve them of pain. They now describe how they had been misled as children and teenagers to see him as a trustworthy savior they could look up to as he consoled them or wiped blood from their injuries.[4]

Suzy is a mother who attended my training and shared a story about her son and his piano lessons. The piano teacher would continuously kiss her son and put him on his lap. Suzy never left her son

---

4- From recorded testimonies in the trial of Larry Nassar.

unattended during the piano lesson. She was offended by the piano teacher's behavior but never said anything. One day, her husband sat in on the piano lesson. The father was able to witness the incident himself and noticed that the kissing bothered his son. "Enough," the father told the teacher. "Don't kiss my son ever again."The son glanced at his father with love and respect. He later told his dad, "You are my hero. You saved me. I hate this teacher." This father built bridges of trust with his son. If anyone's actions ever bother the son again, he knows he can trust his dad to protect him.

The point of these stories is not to make us suspicious of every person we meet, but they do illustrate a real problem. We need to pay attention to those who work with our children: teachers, coaches, and everyone else in their lives.

The SKIT Method

We train children with something we call the SKIT method. It teaches them four important actions and attitudes for preventing abuse:

Say no

Keep private parts private

It's not your fault

Tell someone

Say no
Keep private parts private
It's not your fault
Tell someone

It's imperative to teach our children that no one should force them to do anything that makes them feel uncomfortable. If children feel uncomfortable, they should immediately speak up because these people know how to trick them into sexually abusive situations. Our children are smart enough to get it: to say no, to keep their private parts private, to know it is not their fault, and to tell someone they trust about the abuse. We always tell children that if the first person you report to does not believe you, keep telling people until someone believes you and takes action to protect you.

One of my clients, Melissa, told me a great story:

I am trying to teach my 4-year-old daughter that if anyone comes near her and touches her in a way that bothers her or makes her feel uncomfortable, if anyone tries to pull her pants down, she needs to scream, walk away, and report it to me immediately. One day at the mall, my daughter told me that a boy bit her in her mouth. She didn't understand what the boy was actually doing. All she understood is that this boy bit her. I told her, "Come! I'm going to show you what I'll do to this boy. I will defend you."She pointed the boy out. Mall security intervened and kicked him out of the shop. My daughter was elated because I was able to protect and defend her. Children will report abuse when they feel heard, believed, and protected. When my daughter reports these types of incidents to me, I praise her and reward her so she will be encouraged and continue to confide in me without being afraid.

This mother is an excellent example of parents who make their children conscious of the fact that no one is allowed to touch them in a way that makes them feel uncomfortable. It might not turn out to be abuse, but the response builds trust between parent and child.This parent's response to the incident was ideal. We need to encourage children to report to us if they experience such happenings without fearing that their parents might yell at them or, worse yet, blame them or call them liars.

3

13 Reasons Why: Consequences of Abuse

You can choose to look away, but you cannot say you didn't know.[5]

I know a girl who told her mother when she was 4 years old that someone had kissed her in a way that bothered her. The mother was enraged. She called her daughter a liar and a drama queen. Four years later, the girl was sexually abused by her cousin, but she never told her mother. She expected the same reaction.

This girl is now 25, still suffering from the consequences of the abuse she experienced when she was 8. Sexual abuse has long-lasting effects. Very often, the reaction of a parent or caregiver to reported abuse determines how long-term those consequences can be.

5- William Wilberforce . "On the Horrors of the Slave Trade," speech delivered in the House of Commons, May 12, 1789.

Sexual abuse has many consequences. It affects behavior. It steals hope; a victim may have little motivation for living. It undermines self-esteem; a 17-year-old girl who had been abused many times told me she was from a different breed of human beings, made from the clay of abuse. It instills fear; many survivors live with the fear that any relationship will end in abuse. Many survivors of abuse become controlling and aggressive; they felt out of control when the offense happened, so control and aggression become unconscious ways of defending themselves.

Many victims turn to homosexual lifestyles because their sexual desire was aroused at an early age by being groomed and abused by the predator. The child later shapes his or her sexual identity around this experience. Because a predator verbalizes the abuse as an act of love, a victimized child may have difficulty distinguishing between love, intimacy, and sex, even when the abuse was painful. The child grows with the understanding that love and sex are the same thing.

At one of the schools where I conducted a training, I heard a conversation between two 8-year-old students. Bob asked Michael, "Does your grandpa love you?"

"Yes, of course he loves me!" Michael answered.

"Does your grandpa touch you in your private parts when you spend the night at his place?" Bob explained that his grandfather did that to make him relax and go to sleep.

"No, he doesn't do that with me," Michael said.

"Then he doesn't love you," Bob told him.

When Michael went home, he told his mother he was upset that his grandfather didn't love him.

"Why do you say that?" she asked him. "You know grandpa loves you very much."

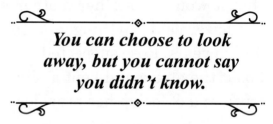

You can choose to look away, but you cannot say you didn't know.

Michael told her what his friend had said. Bob had begun to equate love with abuse and is very likely to grow up having multiple sex partners in order to experience "love" as he has known it.

Some victims learn to hate sex because of the negative emotions associated with it. In a significant percentage of victims, the abuse produces feelings of self-loathing, which is acted out in cutting and other harmful behaviors. Victims can feel responsible for the abuse and punish themselves for what happened to them.

Rose was a beautiful 6-year-old girl when her divorced mother married an abusive man. At first, he was abusive to Rose's mother and treated Rose like a princess. He bought her gifts, and for the first time, she felt that someone cared for her. One night, thunder and lightning from a storm terrified Rose. Her stepfather offered to sleep with her to ease her fears. The idea of having him in her bed made her feel so safe. But he started touching her in a way that made her feel dirty and uncomfortable. She realized something was wrong, but she also knew that it would upset her mother if she told her. So she never said anything, and the abuse continued for ten years. Rose suspected that her mother knew about the abuse and kept a blind eye, afraid of the truth and of losing her provider.

Rose tried to take her own life when she was 16 by swallowing ten of her mother's sleeping pills. Her mother found her on the floor and rushed her to the hospital. Eventually, the mother divorced her abusive husband. Two years after the divorce, I saw the mother at church. She was devastated. She had discovered that her daughter was cutting. Rose had written "I hate me" on her forearm, and when her mother saw it, she realized her fears about her ex-husband's abuse of Rose were justified.

The mental strain of abuse often leads to depression, anxiety, and other disorders. Studies have shown that sexual exploitation can lead survivors to drinking as a way of coping. Harassed women are also more likely to develop eating disorders.

Survivors often loathe their bodies because they think they invited or encouraged the abuse. Victims may subconsciously begin to eat a lot to gain weight, either to become undesirable to the perpetrator or to regain the sense of control that he or she lost during the abuse.Many become anorexic or bulimic.

According to Dr. Rebecca Thurston, who published her cardiovascular findings in the scientific journal Menopause,"People need to understand that trauma is not just something that happens in a survivor's mind. It has real implications on the body."[6]

In more than a dozen other studies, researchers have documented other physical symptoms caused by sexual harassment, such as headaches, gastrointestinal problems, and disrupted sleep.

"People often think of harassment as a single event, but much more commonly, it's a process that happens over time. You keep going to work day after day while this stuff keeps happening," said Louise

---

6- "Researcher Finds Link Between Traumatic Events and Future Heart Disease Risk in Women," PittWire, Tuesday, December 12, 2017. Accessed April 14, 2018, at https://www.pittwire.pitt.edu/news/researcher-finds-link-between-traumatic-events-and-future-heart-disease-risk-women.

Fitzgerald, who has studied harassment in utility workers, office settings, and factories. "It's that prolonged exposure to stress that turns into a physiological reaction."[7]

A 2005 study published in the Journal of Business and Psychology found that those who experienced sexual harassment were more prone to sickness, illness, or accident, and not only around the time they encountered the harassment. A survey of the group years later showed that the harassment continued to have an enduring effect on their rates of illness, injury, and accident.

The physical consequences are only one aspect of sexual abuse. Among the most debilitating effects is post-traumatic stress disorder, and feelings of guilt and shame that continue to hound the survivor are as severe as the physical consequences.

A child sees adults as god-like, and everything they do and say is right. If adults don't love the child, the child assumes it must be his or her fault for being unlovable. If they hurt the child, it's his fault; he must deserve it. If he is in pain, it's his fault; somehow he messed up. It is then a small step for him to draw broader conclusions:

If I'm in pain, it is somehow my fault.

7- Maine Employee Rights Group, "New Study Adds to Body of Evidence that Sexual Harassment Causes Physical Harm," February 15, 2018. Accessed April 14, 2018, at https://www.maineemploymentlawyerblog.com/2018/02/new-study-adds-body-evidence-sexual-harassment-causes-physical-harm.html.

If an adult is hurting me, it's somehow my fault. I messed up.

If I do better, they won't hurt me anymore.

Abuse makes the child put on what we call "abuse spectacles." This becomes his or her window to seeing the world.

Since abuse happens in a dysfunctional setting, there will be layers of other dynamics of abusive behavior as well. The abuser may openly blame the victim for the abuse:"You want this." "Because you are _____, it makes me want it." The abuser has projected his own desires on the victim and avoided taking responsibility for them by transferring the blame to the victim. If this starts when the victim is very young, the child has no other point of reference for truth and believes what the adult tells him. If it doesn't match what he feels, he assumes his feelings are wrong. He learns not to trust his own feelings and intuition about the situation. The victim cannot even seek help because he feels guilty for the situation. It is the abuser's guilt, but he has conveniently given it over to the victim to carry.

This shame is genuine for the victim. It can be reinforced among family members, if they dare to talk about it, and tragically it can be reinforced if the victim does muster his courage to talk to someone outside the family system and is heard only by the "passive bystander" who does nothing about it.After a while, the survivor begins to believe that he really is to blame for the abuse.

If the predator takes time in grooming the child for abuse, the child's body may react to the stimulation,increasing the feeling of guilt and shame. He or she thinks, I am truly a bad person! I deserve all that is happening to me! Or, Is there something about me that will make people not want to connect with me?[8] The child is less able to interact with society and begins to suffer from self-hate.

The child begins to connect some behaviors to feelings of guilt and shame—perhaps becoming secretive, too embarrassed to engage in sports, no longer performing well at school. He or she may find it difficult to form healthy relationships.

Beth actually excelled at school, but no one knew anything about her family. School was her only breath of fresh air. She would not let anyone walk her to her home, where the man who was renting the family's basement was abusing her. He threatened to kill her dog if she told anyone. She was also afraid for her younger sister, so she kept the secret. When she closed the door of her home to go to school, she became another person: the person she wanted to be.

8- Brené Brown, The Price of Invulnerability, Ted Talk, October 12, 2010.

When I met Jeannie at 18, she had already had three plastic surgeries. She always felt that the next operation would make her look as beautiful as she dreamed of being. She wore extremely provocative clothes and had already had multiple sex partners. Through the course of counseling, she revealed the abuse she suffered at a sleepover birthday party. It only happened once, but that was enough to make her feel guilty ever since.

These are not hopeless situations, however. The picture is not always black. Kevin, who was able to overcome abuse and live a normal life, tells his story:

I was sent to an orphanage when I was 2 years old. My father, who was an alcoholic, returned drunk one night and murdered my mother in front of my own eyes. When I was 7, I liked to listen to music, but we were not allowed to turn the music on at any time. We had to have the permission of an older boy. When I asked to turn on the music, he would ask me to do favors for him that I did not understand at first. It went on to become a full-blown sexual relationship. I still didn't get it. When I complained to the supervisor, the supervisor slapped me on my face as if it was my fault. This went on for several years, and I was afraid to speak up again. The only time I felt loved or cared for was during this relationship with this older boy. I was angry with God because I didn't know why I was born or why I was in this dreadful place. I ran away from the orphanage. I slept on the streets. Then I found a home for immigrants.

I started thinking, Is this what my life will be like? What can I do to help myself? I started doing odd jobs and decided to see a counselor. I saw six counselors, but none of them could help me. Then I found a counselor who understood where I came from and what I've been through, and for ten years, he counseled me. He accepted me just as I am, never judging me. He was able to understand that I am not responsible for what happened, but that I also have a responsibility now. What would I do with what happened? Would I waste my pain? Would I continue living in the past or embrace the future?

Today, I am married to a beautiful wife and have two lovely daughters. I believe that now I know how to bring up my children. I have learned how to love and protect my daughters with a love I have never received or experienced. I can enjoy my wife. I don't detest my past anymore. I will not waste my pain.

This is a painful story, but it is also a story of victory. Kevin was even able to forgive the boy who abused him. Stories with happy endings like these show that the world is not dark, that there is always hope for recovery, and that the possibilities for healing are real.

4

It Is Never the Victim's Fault: NEVER

S hame is called the rupture of the self with the self, like internal bleeding of the soul. In working with people who have been abused, we have to emphasize again and again something they internalized at the time of the abuse, sometimes at a very early age: It is never the victim's fault. Never.

That is why my nonprofit organization is called Not Guilty—to emphasize that the victim is never at fault and to undermine the shame that victims often feel.

Eric Spady summarizes his teaching on guilt and shame by asking and answering this question: "How did you learn to be so ashamed?"[9]

This question undermines shame at two levels. On the first level is the release that comes when

9-Eric Spady teaching at Middle East Sexual Abuse Related Pastoral Care (MES-ARPAC), Egypt, 2009.

we reconnect the feelings of shame with the specific memories of personal harm. On the second level, in the act of searching for the learning, a person takes on the definition of shame as acquired rather than inherent. This is contradictory to the whole shame experience because shame is felt as fundamental to one's identity. In effect, a person can hardly look for how he or she learned to feel ashamed and feel ashamed at the same time.

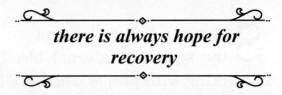

there is always hope for recovery

Painful feelings like grief, rejection, or anger are often first experienced as shame or are covered by a shame response.

"Do you think it's not okay to feel pain instead of shame (i.e., to grieve)?" I ask my patients.

Shame says: I am bad, unworthy of love, unfit. Whatever treatment I get is okay because, after all, it's just me.

Shame walls the heart from receiving love.

Shame happens whenever we judge ourselves unfit in some way.

Shame occurs when our needs as a child are not met (or we are even shamed for having them).

Shame occurs when the abuse destroys self-esteem (sclf-blame).

Shame happens when the abuser's shame/mindset is internalized.

Shame occurs when the abuser disowns guilt and blames the victim.

Shame happens when the child experiences a profound sense of helplessness.

Shame happens when the child assumes responsibility or false guilt for the abuse.

5

Translate the Signs: The Red Flags of Abuse

"Closeness isn't safe. Trust isn't safe."

E very morning before I leave the house, I check the weather report. It determines what I'm going to wear, whether I need to take an umbrella with me, and if I'll need a jacket or boots. Similarly, we as parents need to determine the weather with our children's moods and behaviors. We need to learn how to spot the signs of abuse early on. The earlier we detect them, the easier they are to handle.

Notice any change in behavior. For example, if a child who used to love school all of a sudden hates to go, ask yourself why. What happened? If a child who used to enjoy playing soccer now hates it, ask yourself why. What changed? Notice when your daughter suddenly does not want to wear dresses, only pants; if your child no longer wants to go to a place she used to enjoy; if he starts having recurring nightmares; or if she starts talking about being bad or ugly. Some of these may simply be signs of changing preferences or normal discouragement, but they may point to much bigger issues. Ask yourself what happened. Any change of behavior should raise red flags—not necessarily of abuse, but of the possibility that something is wrong. Learn how to read the weather.

Sometimes parents don't notice the signs because we don't know what to look for. Sometimes we may have suspicions, but because we don't understand how we need to deal with the situation or would be ashamed of it, we ignore it or we try to cover it up and pretend it's not happening. But if a child suspects that his or her parents know about the abuse and are not addressing it, the parents have lost the child's trust, maybe for life.

During a training session for trainers at our Not Guilty office, Scott shared this story:

We were at a church camp. I was preaching, and my daughter, who was 8 years old at the time, was playing in the campsite. During my preaching, she came in running, her face sweaty and flushed. She looked outraged. But I shoved her off and signed her to keep quiet until I finished. When I finished preaching, she told me that as she was buying ice cream, the vendor pinched her in her private part. I did not react at all when she told me. Later, and unbeknown to my daughter, I reported that vendor, and he was dismissed from camp. But I never communicated to my daughter what I had done—that I reported the incident and protected her, as she should expect of me as her father when she faces harm. From that day, our relationship changed. She did not confide in me anymore. As soon as she turned 16, she wanted to go to the college that was farthest from home. I am so sad it has come to that.

I encouraged Scott to write his daughter a letter to tell her what he did—to let her know that he had believed her and defended her that day when she needed a protector. He was concerned that it would not make a difference after all these years, but it might. And it certainly couldn't hurt. Our children need to know that we will protect them in case of harm. Being passive is not an option.Although the signs of abuse aren't always visible, learning what they are could be lifesaving.

The following signs are red flags and may create suspicions that sexual abuse is happening. These signs don't necessarily mean that the person was exposed to abuse beyond the shadow of a doubt. Sometimes we read a book and find that our child has a few of the signs, and we assume that the child is a victim. Many times there could be other reasons for the unusual behavior. But when abuse happens, children are confused. Most have likely been told to obey adults, but their experience at the hands of an adult seems wrong. Was it right to obey in that situation? Is that what love looks like? These questions create enormous stress for a child, and stress manifests in a variety of ways. Look for these signs:

Closeness isn't safe. Trust isn't safe.

• *Regressing to infantile behavior,* like wetting the bed. Not every child who wets the bed is abused, of course. There can be a lot of reasons. But this does suggest that something is disturbing the child—perhaps as normal as mom having a new baby, but perhaps as upsetting as abuse. If wetting the bed is not a medical condition, it is generally a cry for attention.

• *Having nightmares.* Again, there are a lot of reasons for having nightmares, but do take them seriously. This can be one of the earliest signs of abuse. Do not dismiss them or make fun of the child. Children cannot compute life like adults do, and their stress may come out in their sleep. Nightmares may be repetitive, with the same person—in this case, the abuser—repeatedly trying to harm the child and the child running away. I have found that asking children to draw what they have dreamed helps them talk about it.

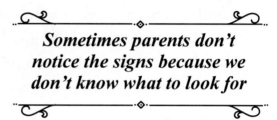

Sometimes parents don't notice the signs because we don't know what to look for

• *Fear of undressing or changing clothes.* A child might become overly conscious about his or her body and anxious about removing their underwear and smelling it.

• *Feeling the need to shower excessively.* A child often feels dirty because of what happened and will want to shower often.

• *Feeling guilty or fearful.* A girl who remembers that she was wearing short clothes when she sat on an abuser's lap might start blaming herself and feeling guilty. Her sense of right and wrong is distorted. Was the adult's behavior good or bad? Was she good or bad? She doesn't know, and she becomes fearful and angry. She is afraid of the perpetrator and afraid that her parents might discover what happened and blame her for it. A child with those kinds of thoughts is in turmoil.

• *Difficulty in trusting others.* Abused children find it hard to trust others, and distrust becomes a way of life. They lose trust in their parents if they believe their parents know and did nothing to protect them. They lose faith in God and wonder where he was when it happened. And they lose trust in people around them, becoming afraid to make close friendships that might uncover their secret and lead to rejection.

• *Changes in eating patterns.* A child may either start overeating or stop eating. During abuse, a child experiences a sense of being out of control. Overeating or refusing to eat is an effort to regain control. Many eating disorders have a root in sexual abuse.

Jane was a beautiful 16-year-old girl who came for counseling for bulimia (eating and then throwing up). She told stories about her mother being jealous of her for being young, thin, and beautiful. Jane said she could never find the clothes she bought after a shopping trip because her mother would take them and wear them. It was clear that she had a lot of anger toward her mother.

Six months into counseling, Jane told me about a science teacher who had insisted on kissing her on the mouth, which made her feel very angry. Not able to stand up to the teacher, Jane told her mother. Unfortunately, the mother just brushed Jane off and took the matter lightly. Neither she nor her mother ever brought it up again, and Jane continued to be abused for six years. Her anger at her mother came from her feelings of being unprotected.

William, a 4-year-old boy in a nursery, always ate a certain amount of food for lunch. One day after finishing his regular portion, he asked the teacher for more. So she poured a second serving. William gobbled it up and asked for more. She gave him a third serving, and William devoured it again. The teacher refused to give him another serving, and when his mother arrived, William threw himself on the floor and broke down. "Don't bring me here again because they don't feed me!" William's real concern was not about food but that the security officer at the nursery had been abusing him. He showed his stress by changing his eating habits.

Amy had a problem with her twins. The man who was renting the family's basement was amiable and helpful. He offered to babysit the boys when Amy had to run errands. Being a single mom, she jumped at the offer. But both children began to lose their appetite. Amy was not aware of the symptoms of abuse and assumed that her twins did not like the kind of food she cooked. She started giving them vitamins to increase their appetite. Only later did she discover they had been sexually abused.

Leaving our children unsupervised for long periods of time is not an option. That's one reason my husband and I would not let our sons go to sleepover parties. I lost count of how many disagreements I had with my two boys over this issue when they were growing up, but I could never be sure who would be there. My father always told me, "Laila, you can never be too careful with your kids."

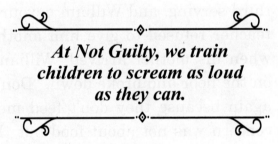

At Not Guilty, we train children to scream as loud as they can.

We also have to teach our children how to respond. At Not Guilty, we train children to scream as loud as they can. We prepare them to say, "This is wrong! I'm going to tell my mom!" We tell them to run, and that they are right to do so. We try to program their thinking in such a way that when abuse happens, they will not have to figure out what to do. They will just know. Too many children struggle with whether they should speak up or not, or whether an adult's actions are right or wrong. We want the message to be ready in their minds so they can blurt out without thinking, "This is wrong. I'm going to tell."

The perpetrator, who is likely brilliant at keeping secrets, will never again try to groom or abuse a child who has threatened to report the abuse. Abusers want to stay in the shadows.

Building bridges of communication between you and your children will result in a better relationship, and it may prevent lifelong scars

It is crucial for parents to keep their eyes wide open and not trust people easily. Observe your children, maintain bridges of trust, and communication openly. These things are not written to instill fear or create alarm. They are meant to inform so that when warning signs appear, parents will look into them further. Watch for those signs. Learn how to intervene intelligently and safely. Do not rebuke your children for what they say. Building bridges of communication between you and your children will result in a better relationship, and it may prevent lifelong scars.

Summary

Here is a list of many of the warning signs of abuse:[10]

Behavioral symptoms

- Exhibiting signs of depression or post-traumatic stress disorder

- Expressing suicidal thoughts, especially in adolescents

- Self-harm

- Developing phobias

- Having trouble in school, such as absences or drops in grades

- Changes in hygiene, such as refusing to bathe or bathing excessively

- Returning to regressive behaviors, such as thumb sucking

- Running away from home or school

- Being overly protective and concerned for siblings, or assuming a caretaker role

- Nightmares or bed-wetting

- Inappropriate sexual knowledge or behaviors

10- Adapted from information provided by Rape, Abuse & Incest National Network (RAINN), https://www.rainn.org/warning-signs.

Verbal cues

- Using words or phrases that are "too adult" for their age, unexplained silence, or suddenly being less talkative

Physical signs

- Bruising or swelling near the genital area, blood on sheets or undergarments, or broken bones

6

Why Don't Children Report?

Statistics indicate that only 10 percent of survivors of sexual abuse report what happened. This means that 90 percent of cases are unreported. Yet one in every six girls and one in every eight boys will be sexually abused before the age of 18. About 30 percent of sexually abused males will become abusers themselves. These are scary numbers.

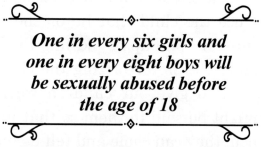

One in every six girls and one in every eight boys will be sexually abused before the age of 18

Why do victims of sexual abuse generally prefer not to report the abuse? And if they do not report, are they not partly to blame for the problem?

Victims of abuse are groomed not only to be abused but also to accept it. Just as offenders lure children by grooming them, parents need to "groom" their children not to accept abuse by making them aware of the lies predators use to keep their acts a secret. These lies include statements like these:

"No one will believe you!"

"You wanted this. See how your body reacted?"

"You made me do it."

"If you tell your mom, she will beat you to death!"

"I will kill your parents if you tell them anything!"

"I'll kill you if you say anything!"

"I will tell your parents you are doing drugs or alcohol."

An offender might even do something to convince the child that he or she will carry out the threats—perhaps by killing the child's pet, for example, thus terrorizing the child into silence. We need to give our children warnings about what might be said to them so that if these things happen, they can come and tell us immediately.

One of the most significant signs of abuse is the feeling of guilt that somehow the child is responsible for the abuse. The perpetrator often plays on this guilt, suggesting that the child should be ashamed of what is happening because somehow it is his or her fault. The abuser says things like, "Look at what you are wearing. See what you made me do?" Carrying the blame, the victim does not want to report and cause trouble.

Another way to exploit a child's guilt or shame is to allow him or her to do drugs, drink alcohol, or watch pornography. Then if the child wants to expose the abuse, the perpetrator can threaten to tell his or her parents of all the shameful secrets that have been going on.

Sometimes the child does not want to lose his or her relationship with the offender or miss out on the attention he or she has been receiving. This is especially true in the case of offending family members; the family might actually blame the child for the loss of the relationship or for the family member being put in jail. One of my clients was told by her father, "What would you do without me if I went to prison? You wouldn't be able to survive. You would starve."

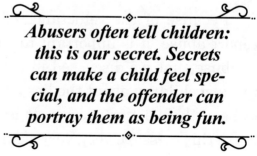

Abusers often tell children: this is our secret. Secrets can make a child feel special, and the offender can portray them as being fun.

Abusers often tell children, "This is our secret."

Secrets can make a child feel special, and the offender can portray them as being fun.

Some children fear, often quite legitimately, that they may be accused of lying if they report an abuse. Some do not report to avoid being stigmatized as a victim of abuse or rape. They have gotten the unfortunate message that society punishes survivors as much as or more than it punishes offenders.

It is important also to make this message very, very clear: when you come and tell me, I will always believe you.

In counseling, I have repeatedly had to tell children, teens, and adults to repeat these words during every session: "You are not guilty. It was not your fault that this happened to you. You are not to blame."

Because of the reluctance of many victims to report abuse, it is important to watch for the signs of abuse that we discussed in the last chapter and to warn children about the lies an abuser might use to keep their actions secret. It is important also to make this message very, very clear: "When you come and tell me, I will always believe you." Remember that children are not likely to make things like this up. Even if they do, every report needs to be investigated because there is a good chance it is true.

Sara's daughter Ella was in third grade. One day Ella told her that the teacher frequently dismissed all of the students after class except her. When everyone had gone, he would make her sit on his lap and try to touch her private parts. When Sara heard this, she yelled at her daughter and called her a drama queen. "You always make stuff up to attract attention," she told her. "You are deplorable. Why are you always doing stuff like that?"Sara assumed that the teacher, who was like a father to her, was just patting her on the back and that Ella didn't understand.

A few years later, when Ella was in sixth grade, she had a private math tutor. At a certain point, Elladid not want to go to her tutoring session and started crying every time Sara tried to drop her at the tutor's house. Sara told Ella that she was an ungrateful brat. After all, Sara was paying good money for this private tutor. Sara kept asking Ella why she didn't want to go to tutoring,but Ella wouldn't tell her. One day, Sara overheard Ella talking to one of her girlfriends on the phone. "My mother is pressuring me to know why I don't want to go to the math tutor, but I cannot tell her since she did not believe me when it happened when I was in third grade." When Sara found out that the tutor was abusing her daughter, she was so sad. She had caused her daughter to be exposed to sexual abuse again, and her daughter did not trust her enough to tell her.

Many adolescents do not report abuse because they are afraid of breaking up their family or being sent to a foster home. It's also difficult for a young person to go against the authority of an adult, especially a parent. It can be hard to come to terms with the fact that the other parent in the household may not believe the truth and deny that the abuse is happening. So many victims of sexual abuse do not report it because they worry no one will believe them. As one anonymous girl testified at Larry Nassar's trial, "If over these many years just one adult listened and had the courage and character to act, this tragedy could have been avoided. I and so many others would have never, ever met you."

Sometimes young people do not report an incident because they think what happened to them isn't bad enough to qualify as abuse. They rationalize. "He was just a friend of the family." "It only happened once." "It was just my older brother, and he was only a year older than me." Sometimes with brothers and sisters who are close in age, both siblings have initiated sexual contact rather than one person holding power over the other. This can cause the same problems as other types of abuse, but the solution is more about healing for both survivors than it is about punishing either of them.

Victims in some instances prefer not to report for fear of the attack they may face from the people closest to them. Rachael Denhollander, a gymnast quoted earlier, put it bluntly:

My advocacy for sexual assault victims, something I cherished, cost me my church and our closest friends three weeks before I filed my police report. I was left alone and isolated. And far worse, I was impacted because when I came out, my sexual assault was wielded as a weapon against me often by those who should have been the first to support and help, and I couldn't even do what I loved best, which was to reach out to others. I was subjected to lies and attacks on my character including very publicly by attorney Shannon Smith when I testified under oath. I was being attacked for wanting fame and attention, for making up a story to try to get money.[11]

Always take reports of potential abuse seriously. Watch out for phrases the child might use

---

11- Rachael Denhollander's full victim impact statement about Larry Nassar can be found at www.cnn.com, January 30, 2018. Accessed April 14, 1018, at https://www.cnn.com/2018/01/24/us/rachael-denhollander-full-statement/index.html.

to try to tell you what is happening, or even questions he or she might ask in order to see your reaction: "What do you think of (name of person)?" "I don't like (name of person) anymore." Or, "(name of person) screams at me, hurts my cat, does terrible things to me," etc.

These are all phrases that should make you stop, listen, and ask more profound questions. They should alert you to something very important that might be going on in your child's life.

7

This Is Us: We Protect Our Kids

"I will educate my children about monsters like you and pray to God they will never experience pain like this." —Olivia Cowan Olympic gymnast

I was invited to give a course on how to protect our children against sexual abuse and harassment. One of the mothers who attended was very disturbed. "It is not possible for us to talk to our children about such things because we will open their eye to stuff they shouldn't know!"she said.

We carried on with the course, and at the end, the same woman came up to tell me that one of her son's teachers undressed the students during break and took pictures of them with his cell phone. I was stunned that the woman who said she doesn't want to open her children's eyes is the same woman who shared this incident with me. I asked if she reported the teacher. She told me she didn't because she didn't want the teacher to flunk her son in school.

"I will educate my children about monsters like you and pray to God they will never experience pain like this."
—Olivia Cowan Olympic gymnast

This mother's personality is divided. How can she not want to talk to her son about sexual abuse issues and at the same time worry that her son may fail school while he is being abused? And which would be a bigger setback—for her son to repeat a school year or lose his life with the long-lasting consequences of abuse, and on top of that, to potentially have nude pictures of him posted on child pornography sites? Though this divide is hard to comprehend, it is not unusual. Many parents are afraid of talking to their children about sex. But if we don't discuss these issues with them, other people will take advantage of their ignorance.

When a child points at his hand or foot, we don't hesitate to give a straightforward answer: "That's your foot." We need to be able to explain body parts and sexual identity to our children the same way. There is nothing wrong with speaking to our children about sex. If we don't give them the sex education they need, they will get it from someone else who distorts it for them. Sex offenders use ignorance against children to abuse them.

Sex education is not a taboo, a sin, or a risk of opening children's eyes or arousing their interests too early. We don't have to be afraid of saying too much, or of not being able to answer questions they ask. The risk is in saying too little. Of course, I am not recommending information overload or giving them age-inappropriate information. I am recommending telling them one step at a time and letting them know they can trust us with their questions.

If we don't offer our children sex education at a young age, someone else will answer their questions. And most of the time it will be the wrong information. Don't leave it to the schools to provide sex education; you never know who will be presenting the information and if they will do it in a way you agree with. Be proactive. Form your own family version of what needs to be said and when to say it.

My husband and I always told our boys that all questions were welcome in our home. There was nothing they could not ask. Some of their questions were embarrassing to me as a mother, but I had the advantage of being a pediatrician, which gave me knowledge and boldness. I had made a decision that whatever they asked, I would try to answer.

When one of my sons was 9, he came home from school with the information that the sex act takes all night. Suppressing a laugh, I asked him where he got his information.

"From friends at school," he said.

"And where do your friends get their information," I asked him. "From their parents?"

"Are you kidding?" he said. "I think you're the only parent in school who speaks to her children about sex so openly."

I wear that statement as a badge of honor. I knew I had succeeded as a parent. I went on to explain the real duration of sexual intercourse. "So when your friends say things like that, tell them you know the truth because your mother is a doctor." Then I ended the conversation with the same sentence I always ended these conversations with: "This is a very safe place to ask whatever you want without shame. If I don't know the answer, I will find out and get back to you. You can ask anything in this house."

I once heard a joke about a father who decided

to talk to his 15-year-old son about the facts of life. He invited his son into his room and closed the door. The father was very nervous, jittery, and sweaty, nervously puffing at his cigarette. He explained that he needed to talk to his son about something very important.

"Go ahead, Dad," his son encouraged. "What did you want to say?"

"I need to talk to you about sex," his father answered.

"Sure, Dad. What would you like to know?"

The story makes us laugh, but it also reminds us that if we wait until our children are too old, it is too late. We need to talk to them as early as 5 years old, and if they start asking questions before then, we need to answer truthfully with just enough information for their age.

> *Sex education does not mean we will only talk about sex. It alsomeans we will teach our children about their sexual identity*

Sex education does not mean we will only talk about sex. It also means we will teach our children about their sexual identity. What does it mean to be a girl? What does it mean to be a boy? What does it mean when we say, "No one should touch you in a way that makes you feel uncomfortable"? What are "private parts"? If we don't teach our children these things, we are neglecting something very important, and someone else will take advantage of our negligence.

Children also learn about life from our reactions as parents. If you are visiting friends and an adult wants to kiss your daughter or son, and your child doesn't want to be kissed, don't say, "Be good, give a kiss." If the child doesn't want to be kissed, it is his or her right to say no. When a parent forces a child to receive a kiss from an adult, maybe because the parent is embarrassed that the child doesn't want to, the parent is sending a message that children should give in to whatever adults ask them to do. That is not the kind of training we want to give.

Children cannot distinguish at an early age what is appropriate and what is not. But when I teach my children to express their feelings and to do what makes them comfortable, they will always come to me and report whatever is upsetting them. The trust relationship I build as a parent with my children will always enable them to let me know when something is bothering them. And it is always better to know than not to know.

What Do We Teach Them?

It is crucial to teach your children that there is something called "good touch" and something called "bad touch." A good touch makes a person feel happy, safe, and protected. A bad touch makes a person feel uncomfortable, ashamed, angry, or dirty.

Teach young children the language they need to talk about their bodies and information about boundaries to help them understand what is allowed and what is inappropriate. These lessons help them know when something isn't right and give them the power to speak up.

Teach your children that there are private parts that can't be touched by anyone or shown to anyone. Teach them that it is their right to say no if someone touched them in a way that offended them or made them feel uncomfortable. Teach your children that if they are in doubt, ask.[12]

What should you say to your children? It depends on their age. If the child is 0-5 years old, a parent needs to label genitals with their proper scientific names. Many of us give genitals bizarre names, which can create embarrassment when they repeat these names in front of strangers or other family members. I don't know why we are

---

12- Not Guilty teaches parents and kids about sex education. There is a book for girls and a book for boys. These books teach both boys and girls that it is their right to say "No!"

embarrassed to give genitals their real names, but it's best to begin with those.

If a child 5-12 years old asks his or her parent questions, those questions should be answered with complete honesty. When my younger sister was pregnant with her first daughter, my 4-year-old son asked her, "How does the baby come out of your tummy?" Later that day, he came and asked me the same question. He told me that he asked my sister. "And how did your aunt respond?" I asked. He said she changed the subject. Even as a 4-year-old, he understood that his aunt didn't want to answer his question. We need to answer our children's questions to gain their trust so that they keep coming back to us if any unfortunate situation happens or if they have any information they need to know.

So how should you respond to your children's questions? First, clarify what they are asking. Ask them what they mean. Ask what they already know about the question. Then you can give complete information and correct any false knowledge they might already have. A 4-year-old girl asked her mother, "Where did I come from?" The mother began immediately to explain to the child about her genitals and the dad's genitals and how parents share one bed. The girl looked at her mother with confusion and said, "Mom! I don't get it. My friend at school comes from England, and my other friend comes from Syria. Where did I come from?" A little clarifying would have helped the mother answer the right question.

If your children have reached puberty, encourage them to approach you with confidence with their questions. Sometimes it is helpful to take the initiative to find out what they already know. Many times, they have gotten wrong information from their friends or from the Internet.

We need to teach our teenagers to have self-respect, respect their body, and respect others. Why is this necessary? Because adolescence is a time of exploration, and dangerous things might happen, like abuse of one child or adolescent by another. If we don't make it a point and pattern to talk to our children from a very young age, it is almost impossible to start talking to them during adolescence, an age known for privacy and silence.

Again, it is the parent's responsibility to educate their children about sex. If you need to gain knowledge, there are many books you can read to educate yourself first before you talk with your child. Sex education is not the school's responsibility. It is not your child's friends' responsibility. It is not the responsibility of the church. Sex education is our responsibility as parents. If we do not take up that responsibility, the percentages of sexual abuse will soar.

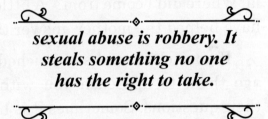

sexual abuse is robbery. It steals something no one has the right to take.

Take the opportunity to build bridges of conversation and trust with your kids. Both you and they need to understand that sexual abuse is robbery. It steals something no one has the right to take. Sexual abuse is selfish because one person gratifies him- or herself while hurting someone else. No one has the right to touch another person without their permission. Make sure your children clearly understand that and can trust you enough tell you when they have been threatened or violated.

Five Questions to Ask Yourself

These five questions, in various forms, have been used by many who work in the field of sexual assault prevention education. 1 Think through them often to see how you are doing in this area of parenting your children.

Are you involved in your child's life? Only by being involved will you see the signs—not necessarily of abuse but of day-to-day changes in your child. You can notice signs of distress, loneliness, fear, and bullying. How many hours a day do you spend with your child? I hate it when parents who do not spend any time with their kids tell themselves they will spend one hour of quality time each day. That's a start, but what kind of impact will you have on your child when you spend only one out of every 24 hours with your child? The child will probably feel more comfortable sharing his or her secrets with the babysitter or teacher who is more available.

When my boys were younger, we had a code that meant he needed my full attention. When he started with the sentence, "Mummy, look at me," I left whatever I was doing to give him my undivided attention. I would kneel down or take him to sit with me on the couch so my eyes and his would be on the same level. Those were the moments he let me into his private world, and if I did not grasp the opportunity to build bridges of trust and friendship, he would never later tell me his deepest secrets.

Do you have a code with your kids? Watch for those special moments when your child opens the door to let you into his or her world. These are precious times when your child decides if he or she can trust you with further secrets and likes and dislikes. These are the moments you will cherish later, when you get a glimpse of what kind of man or woman your child will become. You will get to know his or her fears, aspirations, dreams, and future plans.

Being actively involved in a child's life can make warning signs of child sexual abuse more obvious and help the child feel more comfortable coming to you if something isn't right. If you see or hear something that causes concern, you can take action to protect your child.

Do you show interest in your child's day-to-day life? Some children blurt out everything that happened during the day as soon as they get off the bus. Others are more private; when you ask them if they had a good day, they respond with one or two words and no details. Don't give up on them. Ask open-ended questions. Tell them about your day: what made you happy, who made you angry, how you felt about certain situations. The child will then feel more encouraged to tell you more details about his or her day. Ask them what they did during the day and who they did it with—who they sat with at lunchtime, what games they played after school, if they enjoyed themselves. It's okay if your children share things that might seem petty. Your goal is to encourage them to share anything and everything. When we listen to what is trivial, they learn to trust us with more serious things.

A teacher asked her class to write a paper answering the question,"What would you like to be if you were not a human?" One child wrote, "If I were not a human, I would like to be a TV because as soon as everyone returns home, the TV is on. The whole family sits around watching the TV, and if someone tries to interrupt, everyone else shushes him so they can hear the program they are watching. I wish I were a TV so I could get my father's full attention and he would spend as much time with me as he spends watching TV." When the teacher returned home with the class papers to grade them, she showed this one to her husband.

"How silly," the husband said. "This boy doesn't want to be an astronaut, a doctor, or a performer? He just wants to be a TV?"

His wife looked at him somberly. "This is your son's paper," she said.

Showing interest in your child's day-to-day life is spelled T-I-M-E. The more time you spend with your children, the more impact you will have on them as they grow up. When you invest in spending time with your children as they are growing up, you will have more impact on them when they are adolescents. You will even have more impact on them than their friends do.

Do you know the people in your child's life? Make it your business to know the peers and adults your children spend time with. Ask your child about their fellow students, their friends' parents, and anybody else they may encounter on a regular basis in extracurricular activities—teammates, coaches, members of organizations they are involved with. If you are comfortable talking openly about your children's relationships and associations, they will be more likely to feel comfortable talking about them too.

Choose your children's caregivers carefully. Screen babysitters, staff members of new schools, leaders of extracurricular activities, and so on.

And even after screening, never be too predictable with the caregiver about when you will be gone. Pop in during the middle of the day to see what is going on. Install cameras to see how the caregiver is treating your children.

An excellent book to read with your child are the Not Guilty books for boys and girls. Another good book is Some Secrets Should Never be Kept by Debra Byrne, or I Said NO by Zac and Kimberly King. Books like these should be read at least once a month with the child until the message sinks in.

Watch out for signs of distress. If your child suddenly decides he or she does not like the care-giver any more, you need to ask why. If the child suddenly seems to be scared of the caregiver or too secretive about what they do together, see these as red flags. If you find gifts, toys, or cash with the child and can't account for them, an adult may be grooming him or her for abuse.

As we have seen, perpetrators will often use se-cret-keeping to manipulate children. Let children know they can always talk to you, especially if they have been told to keep a secret. If they see some-one touching another child, they shouldn't keep this secret either. One of the most beautiful things we need to learn is that there should be no secrets between children and their parents. Sex offenders take advantage of communication gaps and barriers between parents and their children, knowing that a child is less likely to report the offense. This is why we need to teach our children never to keep secrets from us parents. Teach them that secrets are different from surprises. For example, if I don't want to tell my mom what I will get her for her birthday, that's called a surprise, not a secret. We need to eliminate the word secret from our dictionary so the offender does not use it to his or her advantage. Teach children that any secrets that make us feel afraid, ashamed, guilty, or uncomfortable should never be kept to oneself. Teach them that reporting something that is happening to another child is not being a snitch; it is keeping that other child safe and could even save that child's life.

Teach your children that the word secret is a bad word when someone uses it against parents. If someone tells your child "Don't tell your mother or father, this is our secret," they need to tell you immediately. Don't overreact. Your response dictates whether your children will continue to confide in you. But do take it seriously.

Do you talk to your children about the media? Media outlets frequently portray incidents of sexual violence in both news and entertainment programs.Talk about these things with your children.

Ask if they have ever heard of these things happening in their lives or among their friends. Ask how they would respond if they saw or heard about these things. Media can be a great prompt to begin a discussion, and your willingness to ask these questions signals to them that these are important issues.

Media exposure can be a good prompt for preparation. Schools conduct fire drills, earthquake drills, and all kinds of emergency preparation. What about a sexual abuse drill? Most people react to dangerous situations by freezing, fighting, or fleeing. No one knows how they will react when put in a dangerous situation, but in many cases, children and adults react by freezing in place, doing nothing—not reacting or running but just standing there. Freezing causes shame and guilt for not reacting. When we train our children on fight and flight (more about that later), we are programming them to react in a way that will keep them safe without having to think.

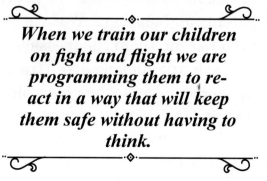

When we train our children on fight and flight we are programming them to react in a way that will keep them safe without having to think.

Do you know the warning signs of abuse? Familiarize yourself with the warning signs of child sexual abuse and be attentive to your child. Even small changes in behavior are worth exploring. Most will probably turn out to be normal—kids often test boundaries and try out new behaviors—but some sudden changes may prove to be significant. Your intervention could make a huge difference in your child's or another person's life.

"I dream that one day everyone will know what the words 'me too' signify," said Aly Raisman at Larry Nassar's trial, "that they will be educated and able to protect themselves from predators like Larry so that they will never, ever, ever have to say the words 'me too.'" Awareness is a good start. Education and open communication are necessary next steps.

Protecting children from sexual abuse is a part of my work. I offer children counseling and training. I have created and taught many kids on how to defend themselves. We provide awareness for parents and teachers. We love our children, and we need to send them the message that we love them. A wise man said long ago, "Train a child in the way he should go, and when he is old, he will not depart from it."[13]

13-Proverbs 22:6, NKJV.

We also need to teach our children that being in groups is safer. Sex offenses are less likely to occur in a group setting. We need to explain to our children not to ask a man by himself for help if they get lost. It's better to ask a mother who has children with her. If a child asks a mother with her children, it is safer than if a child asks a man alone.

We need to explain to our children that they are never to trust an adult who asks a child for directions. Many times an adult will ask a child for directions to lure the child away to a secluded place.

We need to tell our children that we will never send a stranger to pick them up from school. We need to tell them not to get picked up by anyone other than their parents unless we tell them ahead of time that someone else, whom we name, will pick them up. They need to know it is not possible that their mother or father would send a stranger to pick them up.

We also need to teach our children self-defense. When a sex offender sees that a child is confident and is not scared to scream, most of the time the offender will change his or her mind about going ahead with plans for abuse.

Some of these things might seem insignificant, but they might save a child's life. We need to know where our children are at all times. Yes, this is us.

We protect our children from sexual abuse.

Summary[14]

Encourage children to speak up. When children know their voice will be heard and taken seriously, it gives them the courage to speak up when something isn't right.

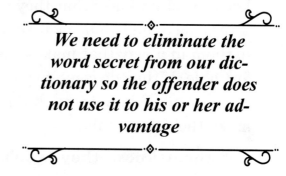

We need to eliminate the word secret from our dictionary so the offender does not use it to his or her advantage

Teach your child about boundaries. Let your child know that no one has the right to touch them or make them feel uncomfortable. This includes hugs from grandparents or even tickling from mom or dad. It is important to let your child know that their body is their own. It is just as important to remind your child that he or she does not have the right to touch someone else if that person does not want to be touched.

Teach your child how to talk about their

14- These suggestions are adapted from the RAINN web site: https://www.rainn.org/articles/how-can-i-protect-my-child-sexual-assault

bodies. From an early age, teach your child the names of their body parts. Teaching a child names of private parts without shame gives the child the confidence to come to you when something uncomfortable or wrong happens to him or her.

Be available. Set time aside to spend with your child when they have your undivided attention. Let your child know that they can come to you if they have questions or if someone is talking to them in a way that makes them feel uncomfort able. If they do come to you with questions or concerns, follow through on your word and make the time to talk.

Let them know they won't get in trouble. Many perpe trators use secret-keeping or threats as a way of keeping children quiet about abuse. Remind your child frequently that they will not get in trouble for talking to you, no matter what they need to say. When they do come to you, follow through on this promise and avoid punishing them for speaking up.

Give them the chance to raise new topics. Sometimes asking direct questions like, "Did you have fun?" and "Was it a good time?" won't give you the answers you need. Give your child a chance to bring up his or her concerns or ideas by asking open-ended questions like "Is there anything else you wanted to talk about?"

8

Hitting the Target

A re some children more vulnerable to abuse than others? Yes. Sex offenders target children who show weakness. We need to strengthen our children so that they are not afraid. We also need to avoid putting them in vulnerable situations. For example, if your child wanted to go to the bathroom at a mall, would you accompany him? Don't send your child to the restroom with a friend or cousin or any other person because restrooms at malls are very crowded and abuse can happen quickly.

Children who feel lonely or who have no friends are easy prey for an abuser. A child might start a friendship with a sex offender because the offender shows interest in him. Whereas the parents may seem too busy to spend time with the child, the predator tries to show the child he or she has plenty of time, and therefore really cares. Many times, a sex offender wants to appear as a regular person that a child knows—perhaps coming to the child's school every day in order not to be considered a stranger. Abusers can be very smart in appearing to show the love and care that the child is not receiving from his or her parents. This is what we mean by "grooming" the child for abuse.

A child who is trusting of strangers is particularly vulnerable to harm. So is a child who accepts emotions, love, and warmth from strangers because he or she doesn't receive these things from his or her parents. And so is a child who feels lonely or deprived, or a child who has no self-confidence and is fearful, or a child whose parents intimidate and instill fear by yelling and hitting. All of these conditions make a child particularly vulnerable to potential sexual abuse.

To prevent your children from being targets for abuse, take care of them. Give them sufficient attention so their "love tank" is full—so they feel loved, accepted, cared for, and wanted in their own homes. When children are sure of being loved and accepted, they are much less likely to search for love and acceptance elsewhere, and the offender will find it much harder to abuse them.
When my boys were young, they loved swimming. We went to the pool almost daily in the summer. I

spoke to them frequently and openly about the fact that they should have clear boundaries, that their private parts were private, and that if anyone attempted to touch them, they should tell me immediately. I always promised they would not get into any kind of trouble since the other party is "the bad guy," as I put it. My mother, who is very conservative, rebuked me. "Why do you tell your boys this stuff? They are too young. Why would you open their eyes to such things?"My answer was, "It is better for me to tell them and keep them safe than for anything to happen and for us all to be sorry."

One hot Monday morning it was 117 degrees, and I was melting, watching my two boys train. I noticed a man wearing a suit and sitting by the pool. I considered it odd that he was dressed in a suit on a sweltering day,but I assumed he must have been one of the parents of the kids in the pool. After swimming,all the boys went to change in the men's changing room. This man went to the changing room and abused several of the boys whose parents had never told them anything about abuse. They were not prepared and did not know what to do. That is why it is so important to teach your children about boundaries and personal space. They need to know that no is a good word.

Strengthen your child's inner self. I found it

very helpful to role-play situations before they happened. Children do not necessarily need to know you are teaching them skills that may help prevent child sexual abuse. What they do need to know is that the information you are sharing with them will give them skills to help keep them safe and healthy.

Never use fear to teach children about safety. This is very important, so be sensitive to how they may perceive your words.

Never use fear to teach children about safety. This is very important, so be sensitive to how they may perceive your words. Scaring them only increases their insecurity and can make them more vulnerable. That can be a difficult balance, but your positive, reassuring approach will help. It is vital to share age-appropriate information that balances protection and empowerment, but without making them afraid in the process.

Prevention education does not harm children. In fact, there is substantial evidence to suggest the opposite. Research shows that children who receive comprehensive preventative training are more likely to report abuse than those who do not. Early disclosure stops abuse from continuing and allows the child victim to get necessary help.

Personal safety should become an integral part of a child's life. It is essential to talk to them matter-of-factly, just like you would approach any other type of personal safety. For example, we teach them to put on a helmet when they ride their bike, to put on a seatbelt in the car, and to lock the door when they are at home. We need to teach them that to avoid sexual abuse, they have to shout, run, and report.

As I mentioned earlier, at Not Guilty we train kids using the SKIT method: Say no; Keep private parts private; It's not your fault; Tell someone. I have even launched a mobile app with a character called SKIT to teach the children how to keep safe through "gamification."It is imperative that kids hear the message many times and in different formats. That's why we use songs, puppets, coloring books, feeling cards, a traffic-light game, and a snake-and-ladder game, all to the effect of making the message stick.

9

Don't Lose Control: What to Do if Your Child Has Been Sexually Abused

One of our biggest fears as parents is seeing harm come to our children—knowing they are unhappy and in pain, and there's nothing we can do about it. As president of Not Guilty, I have counseled numerous traumatized parents and abused children and adults, walking with them on a road to recovery. Recovery can take months or years, depending on the severity of the trauma, the identity of the perpetrator, the length of abuse, and the reaction of the parents when it was reported. When a child reports abuse, what is a parent to do?

There are a few steps we can take to lessen the adverse effects of abuse:

Step 1: Listen. Telling a parent about abuse is not easy for a child. In fact, it can be terrifying, especially if the offender has conditioned him or her to think that no one will believe the child's report.

Step 2: Control your reaction. I realize that hearing such news about your child can be devastating, but his or her welfare at that moment is more important than any emotion you feel. Your reaction at the time of disclosure is crucial. It determines whether your child will feel supported and loved, and often whether he or she will suffer later from post-traumatic stress disorder.

The best reaction, in terms of your tone of voice and body language, is one of compassion, never of anger, aggression, or blame. If you take on the role of a prosecutor, bombarding your child with questions about when and where it happened, why he/she didn't scream, why didn't he/she remember that no one is supposed to touch their private parts, etc., you only make the situation more difficult for your child. Telling you was already hard enough. Let your child tell you at his or her own pace. More details will come out in time. Your child needs to know he or she can trust you to listen compassionately.

Do not feel that you have failed as a parent. That is one of the lies associated with abuse.

Perpetrators can be master manipulators, and many parents miss the warning signs. Don't be too hard on yourself. You can make it through this one day at a time.

Step 3: Don't try to correct the vocabulary. Let your child report the incident to you using his or her own words. This is not the right time to teach the right terms. Just let the child blurt out all that he or she wants to tell you.

Step 4: Believe your child. It's hard for a child to lie about such a matter. If they know about issues of this nature, they have probably experienced them. Parents need to believe what their children are reporting.

Step 5: Show compassion. As mentioned above, compassion is the only appropriate response in this moment. Let your child see it when he or she is telling you what happened. Show empathy.

Step 6: Thank your child for telling you. Let your child know how courageous it was to tell you something so difficult, and that telling you was the right thing to do.

Step 7: Tell the child that it's not his/her fault. Assure your child that he or she is not guilty and that the offender is the guilty one. Becky McDonald, president of Women at Risk International, discussed the phenomenon of freezing with me and explained why it happens so often and produces feelings of shame:

I deal with so, so, so many victims who froze in the face of fear. As you know, one of the results of cortisol when the amygdala senses danger is the fight, flight, or freeze response. The body shuts down to protect. Freeze is a very common response to a sense of danger, and I especially think it is more so with a trusted person. So when the perpetrator is an authority figure, you freeze to process and may not come out of the freeze mode. Those who freeze and do not say "no" struggle for a long, long time with shame. They have been taught to say no but nothing comes out of their mouths. Then they feel that something is wrong with them. Why didn´t they fight?

I spoke at a state university, and in the bathroom was a sign that said, "No answer means NO." It was an anti-rape poster, but it recognized that many do not say no and then are attacked by the court, community, family, etc., for not putting up a fight. In fact, the chemical cortisol (from the flight,fight, freeze place) blocks the prefrontal cortex (the seat of problem solving) so that many cannot move and go into shock and shut down. It is just so, so real. People ask all the time, "Why didn't they run, fight back, yell, or scream?" They assume that normal people do that. Normal people also freeze in the face of danger, and the shame message becomes a resounding gong and deafening drum beat if they finally do tell. So parents need to know that saying "no" may be difficult, and it is actually normal not to. Give children the permission to come to us when they have been hurt, even when they forgot or couldn't say no or didn't know how to fight back. I deal with so many women who get crucified on the stand because they did not say no. They froze in the face of danger and it is viewed as their consent or fault. Not true. I have dealt with thousands of survivors who were silenced very effectively and were never able to get "no" out and feel shamed for that.[15]

Do whatever you can do to release your child from guilt or shame in the aftermath of abuse, regardless of their response at the time.

After following these steps, try to protect the child from experiencing more abuse. Let the child know that he or she will be protected, and then ac-

1- Personal conversation, April, 2018.

tually follow through with protection.

Refer your child for counseling. Be sure that the person treating your child can indeed be helpful because sometimes counselors who are unqualified to address child sexual abuse can actually make the situation worse.

As we have seen, reporting is crucial. Larry Nassar continued to abuse young women for decades because few people reported him, and those who tried to report him were not taken seriously enough. The fact that he was sentenced to up to 175 years in prison means that he was able to abuse numerous athletes on numerous occasions over several decades. He is the perfect model of a pedophile who continues the same behaviors until he is finally caught.

None of us alone can prevent another #MeToo or Larry Nassar. We need each other, and we need to work together to make the world a safer place.